THE UNHAPPY EARL

HENRY WRIOTHESLEY,
THE SECOND EARL OF SOUTHAMPTON

BRYAN DUNLEAVY

THE UNHAPPY EARL

HENRY WRIOTHESLEY,
THE SECOND EARL OF SOUTHAMPTON

BRYAN DUNLEAVY

Published by the Titchfield History Society 2023

ISBN 978-1-915166-06-7

www.titchfieldhistory.co.uk

A catalogue description of this book is available from the British
Library

A Sheltered Life

The second earl, Henry, could hardly have had much memory of his father and was raised by a mother who never remarried and went to some lengths to insulate her son from outside influences. She appears to have resisted any summons to court before 1564 and brought up her son in a highly-protected environment. There were to be consequences.

No-one has recorded the feelings or state of mind of Countess Jane at the relatively early death of her husband at the age of 45. She was herself about 40 years old with three surviving daughters and a five year old son. She was a very rich woman and her 'widow's third' gave her financial independence. Without doubt she would have been an very attractive prospect for men who would be quick to take the opportunity to enrich themselves but she appears to have brushed off any marriage proposals and set about devoting her life to her son. This was entirely laudable, but in retrospect may not have been in the best interests of her only surviving son who grew up without a father figure.

On the death of Thomas Wriothesley in 1550 the earldom passed to his son Henry who had yet to reach his fifth birthday anniversary. In the custom of the day the wardship of the minor passed to the crown to be administered by the Master of the Wards. He in turn sold the wardship to the highest bidder, in this instance Sir William Herbert. The dowager Countess of Southampton had sufficient resources of her own to buy back the wardship from Sir William and proceeded from that point to manage the upbringing of the child.

Jane, Countess of Southampton, was a devout follower of the Roman church. Her husband, although religiously conservative himself, had been more circumspect about his own religious leanings at the court of Henry VIII. Jane Southampton was under no such pressure and made sure that the boy's catholic education was absolute. Within three years, after the death of Edward and the accession of Mary, her commitment to the old church could be open. Five years later, after Elizabeth came to the throne and the Protestants were once more in the ascendant, it became more difficult to be overt in practice, but Elizabeth and her ministers were willing to tolerate private catholicism, provided that it would not jeopardise the state. Thus, the

Countess and her friends were never under pressure to renounce their faith and most likely dreamed of a day when orthodoxy would return.

Countess Jane seems to have been successful in keeping the young Henry away from Protestant influences by bringing him up at Titchfield far away from the pernicious influences of the London court. The boy, with only one parent, was exposed to a world view through his mother's prism. She appears to have been a possessive woman. Not only did she manage to keep the boy away from court but she apparently opposed his marriage to Mary Browne, the thirteen year old daughter of Viscount Montagu of Cowdray Park. This ought to have been highly acceptable as the Brownes were also committed catholics, but perhaps this matriarch had become too possessive. The father of Anthony Browne, Viscount Montagu, was Sir Anthony Browne, a descendant of the great Nevill family through his mother, and several other distinguished lines. He was also the half-brother of William FitzWilliam, who held positions of prominence at the court of Henry VIII and not incidentally was the first holder of the title Earl of Southampton. Fitzwilliam died childless in 1542 and left his very extensive estates, including Cowdray, to Sir Anthony Browne. The fact that Sir Thomas Wriothesley, a fellow conservative and associate of FitzWilliam, took the title of Earl of Southampton in 1547 is perhaps not coincidental. One must suspect that Countess Jane was unwilling to let go. Nevertheless, the 2nd. earl was of age and did not need his mother's permission and they married on 19 February 1566.

> 'Tuesday, 19 February 1566, the marriage was solemnised at London in my lord Montagu's house at his advice, without the consent of my Lady his mother.'

Henry was far too young when his father died to be conscious of the lurch to Protestantism and as he grew in awareness Roman Catholicism was orthodox for five years under the reign of Mary. At her death the young earl was almost a teenager and his character and religious beliefs were fully formed. He was not to deviate from his passionate catholicism for the remainder of his life.

In retrospect, this sheltered life did him no favours. The summons to appear at court in 1564, cited at the head of this chapter, suggests that the countess had been stalling for some time. At the age of 19 his mind was made up, but his beliefs and character and his lack of experience of the political world of accommodation left him ill-prepared for the role that his position demanded of him. Elizabeth and her government took a moderate position and, where possible, steered clear of absolutism. While the country was officially protestant, adherence to the old faith was tolerated provided it did not lead to instability. Most of the peerage were catholic but her pragmatic policy was aided by the fact that many catholics did not want to go back to the turmoil of Mary's years.

Mary Browne, 2nd Countess of Southampton

The young earl inherited his father's intensity, but whereas Thomas was able to govern his temper through his political and careerist instincts, his son lacked that moderating influence. Young Henry, who probably had no memory of his father, was entirely subject to his mother's influence, which in religious matters was pure and unadulterated by political considerations. There were no balancing influences on his upbringing to make him a more temperate adult.

In 1566, the year of his marriage and majority, he came fully into his estates and was immediately a rich young man. His wealth and status would have naturally made him eligible for a place at court and some office in government but he proved unequal to such expectations. Southampton was quickly marked as something of a hothead. It appears that Cecil arranged for the Queen to be hosted by Southampton at Titchfield during the summer of 1569. This did not come to pass because other, more seditious activities were taking place at Titchfield. The Earls of Sussex and Southampton, together with his brother-in-law, Viscount Montagu, met at Place House to discuss how they could support a proposed marriage between the Duke of Norfolk and Mary Queen of Scots. This proposed union was not without support - even Leicester was in favour - and Sussex and Southampton were not out of tune with a large body of opinion. Norfolk was a Protestant and such a union had potential to rersolve the succession issue with a 37 year-old childless and unmarried queen. However, when she learned of the proposal Elizabeth vetoed the proposed marriage.

1569 was a dangerous year. England north of the Humber only had fertile land in the vale of York and on the eastern coast and was at an economic disadvantage to the prosperous south. The population held tenaciously to their feudal lordships and to the catholic faith. So a rebellion in October 1569 led by the northern earls of Northumberland and Westmoreland was serious the Earl of Sussex was sent north to suppress it and within a few months the uprising fizzled out.

Left to their own devices and in the belief that the northern uprising would lead to the regime change they desired, Southampton and Montagu consulted with the Spanish ambassador and with his encouragement decided to support the Duke of Alba, who was engaged in suppressing the Dutch protestants in the Netherlands. It was a fiasco. They set sail for Flanders but the winds were against them and they were forced back to England. By this time the word of their activity was out and once they had landed on English shores they were quickly escorted to the Tower.

Good will was still in plentiful supply. In February 1570 Henry Radclyffe, Earl of Sussex and himself married to one of the catholic Howards, wrote to Sir William Cecil to intervene with the young earl, "that he may be rather charitably won than severely corrected." The Queen and Cecil were prepared to tolerate Montagu and Southampton if they were willing to behave themselves in future. Montagu chose to be loyal. He was made Lord Lieutenant of Sussex and allowed to keep his religion. He never made trouble again and even, when an old man, came to Tilbury in 1588 to defend the crown against the Armada. Southampton, although let off leniently, was not the compromising type. Within a few months he was in trouble again.

In May 1570 he arranged to meet in London with John Leslie, the Bishop of Ross (an agent for Mary Queen of Scots) to seek advice about whether he should continue to serve his queen. In this very month John Felton had pinned to the door of the Bishop of London's house the Bull of Pius V excommunicating the queen. The authorities were on red alert and the earl's attempt to meet with John Leslie took him into very dangerous territory. They agreed to meet across the river on Lambeth marsh, a seemingly obscure place, but they were being watched and were arrested. The two men claimed that they were merely enquiring about the health of Mary, Queen of Scots, at that time under guard at Tutbury Castle but it was a weak and transparent lie.

Once more the Privy Council gave Southampton the benefit of the doubt and in the Summer he was allowed to move out of the Tower to live under house arrest in Surrey. They must have regarded Southampton as a political lightweight, an impulsive hothead with little judgement and no following. He could be, and was, kept under house arrest, as much to keep him from further foolishness rather than constrain a dangerous man. His custodian, Sir William More of Guildford, was instructed to persuade Southampton to take part in household devotions using the book of Common prayer. If he did so, they could then interpret this gesture as conformity with the Church of England. After some resistance Southampton agreed to participate and in November was allowed to go free.

However, his meeting with the Bishop of Ross would come back to bite him. In September 1571, Walsingham's spies uncovered the Ridolfi Plot, which was to raise a catholic army under the leadership of the Duke of Norfolk, and, with the assistance of a Spanish invasion force, overthrow Elizabeth and put Mary Queen of Scots on the throne. Roberto Ridolfi was a Florentine banker with strong connections to the ruling classes and able to travel freely across Europe. He was appointed as an agent by Pope Pius V who was himself dedicated to the overthrow of Elizabeth's government. As with many of these plots the imaginings of the plotters was fanciful. It largely depended on an uprising within the country against Elizabeth and although they might depend on some catholic families like the Wriothesleys and the Brownes, it is far from clear that the majority of the country would wish her overthrow. It secondly depended on an invading force of 10,000 men led by the Duke of Alba, who still had his hands full in the Netherlands. The prospects of this were by no means certain. And finally, Thomas Howard, the duke of Norfolk, was himself a Protestant motivated more by personal ambition than ideology. It was less than certain that many catholics would be willing to risk their lives for a venture with such precarious outcomes.

The Bishop of Ross, John Leslie, as confessor to Mary, Queen of Scots, one of the central characters in this scheme and was arrested and charged. He then, to use a more modern phrase, began to sing like a canary, and amongst other things recounted the substance of his meeting with Southampton. The earl had of course questioned whether he could in conscience show loyalty to Elizabeth. The Privy Council could no longer pass over this treason as the folly of a young hothead and in October 1571 he was arrested and sent to the Tower of London, where he was to languish for 18 months.

After a long period of incarceration he appeared to see the error of his ways and on 14 February 1573 he wrote to the Privy Council to assure them that he was "careful and studious to leave no means undone by all humble and therewith faithful submission and attestation of loyal obedience, to recover her Majesties good grace, opinion and favour towards me".

These were the right words and together with submissions from friends and supporters the Privy Council accepted his contrition and released him once more to the more tolerable custody of William More on 1 May 1573, and later on 14 July to his father-in-law at Cowdray.

In this period his wife gave birth to a son. The date was recorded as 6 October 1573. He now had an heir to his title and some assurance that the Wriothesley line would continue.

The dowager countess, baptised as Jane Cheney and the widow of Thomas Wriothesley, the 1st earl of Southampton died in the year following the birth of her grandson, Henry, on 15 September 1574. She had been a widow for 24 years and by law entitled to one third of the income from her deceased husband's estates and was therefore a rich woman. She had chosen not to re-marry and appears to have lived in considerable style and comfort. Her will made bequests in considerable detail of all the jewellery she had acquired. At her death the one-third of the estate's income reverted to the control of the earl. This windfall may have prompted him to embark of his great Dogmersfield project.

The ruins of Cowdray Palace at Midhurst in Sussex

A Difficult Marriage

The marriage to Mary Browne, a daughter of Anthony Browne and his first wife Jane Radcliffe, herself a daughter of the earl of Sussex proved difficult. His teenage bride, Mary Browne, was pregnant at least three times in the first years of the marriage in between her husband's times in custody. There were two daughters and a son. There may also have been another son but the issue stopped after Henry. Once in her twenties the countess was able to stand up to her difficult, obstinate, wilful, and often bad-tempered husband. One might imagine that after the birth of a healthy son she felt that she had fulfilled her duty and may no longer have been willing to share a bed with her husband. There were rows and perhaps not as many reconciliations as there should have been.

Matters came to a head in 1577 when the earl suspected her of having an affair with a man named Donesame and forbade her to have anything more to do with him. Later, in 1580, there was a breach, or reported breach of this order and the earl erupted with rage. However by this time he was no longer on speaking terms with his wife and communicated with her through an intermediary, usually his steward Thomas Dymoke, whom apparently the Countess could not stand.

An almost blow-by-blow account of this ruction survives in a letter written by the Countess to her father, dated 21 March 1580. Some caution must be exercised here because she only gives her side of the story, but enough can be divined from what else we know about the earl's character for us to piece together the likely course of events.

At the time of the letter the Countess had been banished from the earl's "board and presence" and was living in one of the Hampshire houses separate from her husband. Access to her son was also restricted in that visitors had to seek permission from the earl first. The major charge, that of adultery with Donesame, was a serious one, and she answered it thus:

> And as for the matter charged of Dogmersfield & Donesame his coming thither, he shall never prove it as he would, except he win some to perjure themselves about it. For by my truth, in my life, did I never see him in that house. Neither I assure your Lordship since I was by my Lord forbidden his

company, did I ever come in it. Desire I did to speak with him I confess, & I told yow why and I wished that the cause with my meaning were uttered by the party himself upon his conscience (if he have any) wherefore I coveted to speak with him. And then (I trust) I should be acquitted of greater evil, then overmuch folly, for desiring or doing that, which, being by my enemies mistaken, doth breed this my slander and danger.

It is difficult enough even in contemporary marital disputes to determine the right and wrong of either side, and at a distance of over 400 years and with so little information, impossible to determine who is telling the truth. We do know that the earl was a difficult personality and quite as likely to see offence where none was intended, or to magnify some slight to his honour. Was the countess entirely innocent, or was there a fire behind this little whiff of smoke? A piece of pedestrian rhyme by a poet by the name of John Phillip, *An Epitaph on the death of the Right honorable and vertuous Lord Henry Risley, Noble Earle of Southampton* includes these lines:

In wedlock he observed, the vow that he had made:

In breach of troth through lewd lust, he ne would seem to wade.

Phillip could not claim to know the actual truth but he would have been aware of the gossip of the day and what we may take from these lines is that the gossip concluded that the Countess had behaved inappropriately. This is not to say that common gossip knew the truth. The Countess maintained strong denial at the time and even after the death of her husband.

The consequences were catastrophic for the marriage and must have had some impact on the son. His father's extreme reaction must have indelibly imprinted on the young Henry's mind. As a young boy of 8 he would have difficulty in understanding the sin of adultery and one may be sure that it was not explained by his father in a reasonable or sympathetic way. The countess was never allowed to see her son during the lifetime of the father and unsurprisingly he was never close to his mother. We can suggest that his early rejection of marriage may have had their roots in this experience.

There was also a cooling off of relations between the Montagus and the Southamptons, whether because of this dispute or an earlier cause. The countess's letter to her father suggests that there had been an earlier quarrel between Southampton and the Brownes. We are not on sure ground here but it is plausible. There was also a letter many years later suggesting that Charles Paget, son of Thomas Wriothesley's old colleague, may have contributed to the rift.

> I will overpass his youthful crimes, as the unquietness he caused betwixt the late Earl of Southampton and his wife yet living.

Father Parsons, a Jesuit, writing many years after made this observation:

> One thing also increased the difficulties of the Catholics at this time, which was the falling out between the Earle of Southampton and the Lord Montacute about the Earle's wife.

How this was resolved, if indeed it was, we do not know because there is no further report of the matter and in any case the earl's unhappy life was to come to an end the following year. All that can be added is that she may have had a reasonable explanation for her meeting with Donesame but was traduced by gossip-mongers who had the ear of the earl.

This story tells us is that the earl was an insecure and jealous type and probably susceptible to the idea of anything said against his wife as being proof of her possible infidelity. It is likely that the countess may have harmlessly flirted with this man called Donesame (who figures in no other documents and is never heard of again) and there was no more to it than this other than the earl's initial overreaction.

Unfortunately for his own emotional well-being the young boy Henry was forced to take sides. His father banished his mother in 1579 and it appears that for the last two year's of the second earl's life he would not allow his wife to see her son. She did try to use the boy as an intermediary by writing a letter to the earl to be delivered by her son and although the six year old boy took the letter to his father the earl refused to read it. After this the boy was entirely under his father's influence and unsurprisingly in the circumstances took his side. His mother wrote in a later letter, "he was never kind to me" and we might trace the young Henry Wriothesley's own difficulties with women as a young man to these early experiences.

Mary's unfortunate experience of marriage put her off re-marrying for a long time. She wrote to the Earl of Leicester resolving not to 'put self in the lyke condicion.' Indeed, this comparatively young woman (she was barely 30) did not enter matrimony again until 1594, when she married Sir Thomas Heneage on 2 May 1594. Heneage was by this time an old man, over 60 years old, and indeed he was to die the following year. In October 1594 her son would come fully into his inheritance and she may have been motivated by concerns for her own financial security. Heneage was a Privy Councillor and was well-connected at court. He had been the holder of many offices of state and had himself built up substantial estates. This marriage was his second and his first wife had died in 1593.

It would seem however that the new couple genuinely liked each other and she did care for him in the last year of his life, when he was not a well man. His estate passed to his only daughter from his first marriage and the countess was entitled to her widow's third of the income from Heneage's estate. However he died with heavy debts, which his widow had to pay off over time.

Her choice for a third marriage was William Hervey, a Kentish gentleman who may not have been much older than her son. His date of birth is unrecorded but he was known to be at the court of Queen Elizabeth in 1587 and he distinguished himself on the lord admiral's flagship during the defence against the Spanish Armada in 1599, so we might estimate his birth date at between 1567 and 1570, and therefore only five years older than the third earl at the most. This may have been the reason behind the earl's hostility towards the marriage. He was never on close terms with his mother and on this occasion he made his opposition clear. Eventually the two married in secret, sometime around 1598. Hervey was a capable man and he had served with distinction in several naval engagements. This was Hervey's first marriage and he was marrying a woman old enough to be his mother. No doubt there was some opportunism here; the marriage to a dowager countess had career advantages and indeed he was made keeper of St Andrew's Castle in Hampshire, a post that brought him

£19 3s. 4d. a year. Of course there were no children. Mary died in 1607 and he married a younger woman the following year. She bore three sons and four daughters. Hervey had a good career and became a baron in both Ireland and England. He died in 1642.

LAST DAYS AT DOGMERSFIELD

This early 19th century engraving of the house at Dogmersfield gives us some idea of the general magnificence of the park and the house. It had been the property of the Bishop of Bath and Wells in medieval times and was considered a suitable residence in 1501 for the first meeting of Prince Arthur and Catherine of Aragon. The 1st earl of Southampton acquired the property in 1547 and his son, the 2nd earl started to develop a grand house there in the 1570s. There is no trace of his work since the house was rebuilt along the lines illustrated in the above engravinbg after 1728.

After the birth of his son Southampton ceased to plot against the government and appeared to settle down and attend to his estates. He was given some offices to encourage him in his loyalty; he was appointed to the Commission for the Peace for Hampshire and was later employed to survey the coastal defences. In 1579 he was appointed to a commission for the eradication of piracy. These were not large offices of state but they were signals to the earl that if he conformed he might expect better. It appeared that the earl did stay out of political trouble during these years and instead of fruitless plotting, he set about spending some of his father's inheritance.

Thomas Wriothesley had been a careful manager of money and by this means had built a significant fortune.

After the death of his mother all of the income from the estates ell to him and he set himself the task of creating a great house at Dogmersfield.

We know very little about this project except that it was unfinished at his death and even at his own estimate in his will the work might take up to ten years to complete. This appears to hint at a grand design, possibly one that was very expensive and as I have noted the executors must have abandoned or placed the project on hold. There is no evidence that his son or grandson showed any interest in resuming work at Dogmersfield.

There was a medieval bishop's palace on the site, owned and occupied by the bishops of Bath and Wells since the 12th century at least. At the Conquest it was a royal manor, which was later granted to Ralph Flambard, bishop of Durham. It fell back into royal hands during the time of Henry I, who then granted it to the Bishop of Bath and Wells. There were subsequent disputes about the rights to the manor but Henry II appeared to settle the matter in favour of the bishop. In 1205 King John ordered wine to be sent to Dogmersfield, 'to be placed in the house of the Bishop of Bath' and in 1207 confirmed the bishop's right to the manor. The manor had a good hunting park and was favoured by the bishops, some of whom died there, until the 1530s when Henry VIII took possession.

Some indication of the quality of the residence might be inferred from its choice by Henry VII as a meeting place for Arthur, Prince of Wales and his intended wife, Catherine of Aragon. Catherine had landed in Plymouth on 2 October 1501. It then took 33 days of travel over difficult roads for the young princess to reach Dogmersfield and it seemed proper for the king and her intended husband to make the effort to meet her part way. Ten days later she was able to enter London in the great pageant organised by earl Henry's great grandfather, as recounted in the opening chapter.

Henry VIII at first leased the manor to Oliver Wallop for 21 years in 1542, but on his death, Edward VI granted it to Thomas Wriothesley, 1st earl of Southampton. It is unlikely that the earl did much with his new property in the last three years of his life and there would have been no interest in developing the manor during the minority of the second earl. However, once released from prison the second earl seems to have adopted Dogmersfield as his special project. Almost nothing is known of the medieval bishop's palace. Henry Wriothesley's project must have planned a complete rebuilding of the medieval palace, probably to compete with his father's transformation of Titchfield. The earl was still a young man and with a career at court closed off to him needed some outlet for his energy. In this context the Dogmersfoeld project would give him purpose.

Almost nothing is known about the second earl's plans. Since he anticipated ten years of building we may assume that the project was ambitious, and from 1577 to 1581 he must have devoted himself to it.. The third earl had interests of his own and together with his financial difficulties may have completely ignored Dogmersfield. The 4th earl, when he came to straighten out the affairs of the earldom, sold the estate in 1629 to Edward Dickenson. This then passed to William Godson, descending to a female heiress, Martha, who married Ellis St John. They began to build a new house in 1728 which was enlarged throughout the 18th century.

The Elizabethan manor house, started by the 2nd earl was thus completely obliterated and no drawings survive to tell us what it might have been like.

On the 4 October 1581 the unhappy earl gave up on his short and furious life. He was only in his 36th year. The cause of his death is not recorded although A. L. Rowse describes him as consumptive. It is possible that a bout of pneumonia brought down a body that had already been weakened by the stress of his marriage and his inability to steer clear of seditious activities, and if it was not pneumonia then it was something else. One might note that he was now the third generation of Wrythe/Wriothesleys to die prematurely. William Wrythe, his grandfather, died in 1513, probably in his thirties and his father the first earl only made it to 45. We know almost nothing about William Wrythe but our knowledge of the first earl gives us a highly strung, intense character who was subject to periods of illness, probably at the end of long periods of sustained hard work and it appears that his son Henry, although nowhere near as busy, was also subject to wearing himself thin because of his extreme temperament.

At any rate, for the second time, the earldom fell into the inheritance of a minor.

He died at Itchell House, a few miles away from Dogmersfield, apparently with his son and daughter in attendance and he was buried in Titchfield Church on 30 November 1581. It is not known why six weeks elapsed before he was buried, but perhaps delays were caused by disputes about the will.

The second earl did have time to construct an elaborate will, which was dated 24 June 1581. He was unreconciled to his wife and it contained some vindictive provisions against her. His daughter Mary was given a legacy, but only on the condition that she never be in the same house as his widowed mother. The countess was legally entitled to enjoy a one third share of the estate for her lifetime, so there is nothing the earl could do to countermand that, but in the first will she received nothing more. As he sunk closer to his death the earl adopted a more forgiving tone and added a written codicil to the will. In place of the house at Dogmersfield he offered an annuity of £80 and further, to show the world the he died 'in a spirit of perfect charity' he offered her a bequest of £500. Dymoke did extremely well out of the will. He was given a legacy of £40 and a further legacy of £200. A further £40 a year was granted 'to be attendant dayly about the person of my sonn'. Dymoke got Whitely House and presumably the farmland around it, and when the third earl came of age he was to get Bromwich Farm on a 21 year lease - again adjacent to Titchfield. Dymoke was also one of the executors of the will.

The Countess was not moved by any of this. All of their communication for the past years had been through intermediaries and the earl was obviously too stiff-necked to humble himself through a face-to-face attempt at reconciliation. She immediately set about contesting the will. She wrote to the Earl of Leicester, who was a cousin and then at the height of power and influence. He agreed to assist, but wanted assurance that the new earl was not going to turn out to be a committed papist. She replied that it was not her fault if her son refused to hear the Anglican service because she had not been allowed to see him for two years.

The first result of Leicester's intervention was that the young Lady Mary was restored to her mother's care where she apparently remained until she married. Her next victory was that Thomas Dymoke whom she detested as a man "void of ether wit, ability or honesty" agreed that while he would keep the benefits conferred upon him he would, in effect, step down as executor and stay out of the affairs of her son. He was relieved of his role as administrator of the estate in favour of Edward Gage.

There remains some curiosity about Thomas Dymoke. He was obviously a steward for the earl at Titchfield but he appears to have proved his ability and his functions extended beyond Titchfield. In his will the earl is fulsome in his praise of Dymoke as a man worthy of his trust. He received legacies of £240 and an income of £40 a year, quite substantial sums that would allow Dymoke to live in some comfort.

We can infer that the man was competent and an excellent servant to the earl, helping him manage his complex affairs, which he may not have had the temperament to cope with. Equally plainly the Countess detested the man, but this may be coloured by the fact that he acted as a messenger for her estranged husband. It is curious however that Dymoke has left little trace on Titchfield. The parish registers start in 1589, less than a decade after the earl's death but there is no sign of a Dimmock in any of the variant spellings. Thomas Dymoke was still alive in 1594 and living at Whitely Lodge as he was a participant in the Danvers' affair. After this he disappears without trace. There is no record of his burial in the Titchfield Parish Register, which begins in 1589, nor is there any evidence of wife or children. He may have given his name to Dimmock's Moor near to Whitely Farm. He may have been buried at the nearer church of St Bartholemew at Botley, but there the extant register only starts in 1679, so his end may remain a mystery.

The final extravagance of this will was the expensive tomb which rests today in the parish church of Titchfield. There was to have been two - one for his father and mother and another for himself. He demonstrated a lack of realism. He authorised £1,000 for tombs to his father and himself, an enormous sum. The entire Titchfield Abbey estate was purchased for a sum not far in excess of that amount of money. A further £1,000 was to be spent on his funeral. In addition, he bequeathed £2,000 to his daughter Mary, with the rather spiteful condition that she could not live with her mother.

The splendid tomb at St Peter's Church in Titchfield was provided for in his will and commissioned by his executors. Ther view from this side shows the second earl, in military dress, with his mother on the top tier. His two children, Mary and Henry, are depicted kneeling at prayer. Two tombs were envisioned by the earl, but the executors prudently settled for a single monument.

Bear in mind that the annual income from the land and property he inherited was in the region of £1,300 a year, so in effect he was willing away three years' income in his last desperate moments. It was too ambitious. Once the executors had opportunity to examine the earl's income and debts they wisely decided that both families could be accommodated in a single monument. In addition he charged his executors with the completion of Dogmersfield which he estimated might take up to ten years. Here again the executors concentrated their minds on the possible rather than the fanciful and may have done enough to make the house habitable as it was, without commissioning further expansion. The earl did indicate in his will that the interior walls at Dogmersfield had been plastered, a sign perhaps that a good part of the planned complex was near completion.

The earl pronounced himself in perfect health four months before his early death but one suspects that he must have had some premonition of his early demise. With the exception of his mean-spirited clauses directed towards his wife he showed himself to be generous. Too generous in the opinion of A L Rowse who felt that it was "extravagant with a touch of fantasy about it." His bequests included 100 marks to be distributed in alms at his funeral, £200 to be distributed to the poor on his estates and £3 each to every almshouse in London and Hampshire. These were not small sums of money. £1,000 was to be spent on the two tombs already mentioned and to make substantial improvements to the parish church at Titchfield.

This monument, housed in a chapel at St Peter's church in Titchfield, is the second earl's greatest legacy.

Viscount Montagu was one of the executors of Henry Wriothesley's will and took the opportunity to commission his own family tomb from the same workshop. It was installed in the church at Midhurst. In 1851 it was decided to move the monument to St Mary's Church at Easebourne. Unfortunately the monument could not be fitted in the new space and the obelisks at each corner (similar to those at Titchfield) were cut away.

FURTHER READING

The second earl only lived to the age of 36 and his insistent Roman Catholicism excluded him from statesmanlike roles. Ther most detailed account of his married life can be found in

> C. C. Stopes, The life of Henry, third earl of Southampton, Shakespeare's patron (1922)

In addition, he has a short biography in the Oxford Dictionary of National Biography.